THE GREAT FORT WAR!

FRIENDS, FOES AND ADVENTURE

SEAN P. KRAMER

TABLE OF CONTENTS

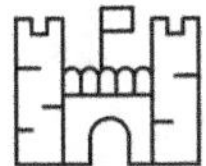

CHAPTER 1

THE FIELD OF DREAMS

Summer had just begun, and the four friends—Max, Sam, Javi, and Jennifer—were restless. School was out, the days stretched on forever, and they needed a place to call their own. A place where they could have adventures.

Max, the leader of their small group, squinted against the sun, his wild brown hair sticking up in all directions. "We need to find a spot. Somewhere no one else goes."

They were sitting on the curb at the end of their street, their legs dangling as they stared out at the familiar houses and yards. Their neighborhood was nice, but predictable. They had ridden their bikes up and down the same roads, played the same games in the park, and now they wanted something new. Something bigger.

Javi, ever the thrill-seeker, was bouncing on the balls of his feet, unable to sit still. "I heard there's an old construction site past the creek," he said, twirling his bike around in the dust. His voice held a hint of mischief, the kind that always got them into the best adventures. "Nobody goes there anymore."

Sam frowned, adjusting his glasses nervously. He was always the careful one. "Isn't that dangerous? They were supposed to build houses there, right? What if there's... I don't know, leftover stuff? Rusty nails? Broken glass?"

Max grinned, nudging Sam with his elbow. "That's what makes it an adventure! Come on, Sam. Where's your sense of fun?"

Sam shifted uncomfortably, but even he had to admit the idea of an abandoned construction site was intriguing. He had spent enough time reading about explorers and adventurers to know that the best discoveries often happened when you least expected them.

Jennifer, who had been standing with her hands on her hips, already seemed to have made up her mind. "We should check it out. If it's as cool as Javi says, it could be our new spot for the summer."

Max jumped up, his energy contagious. "Let's go then! Last one there has to carry all the water bottles tomorrow!"

With that, Max was off, leaping onto his bike and pedaling furiously down the street. Javi followed close behind, his laughter echoing through the neighborhood as he sped after Max. Jennifer gave Sam a quick smile before hopping on her bike and taking off, her blonde ponytail flying behind her.

Sam sighed, knowing full well he'd be the last one. Still, he couldn't shake the excitement bubbling in his chest. Maybe this summer would be different after all.

The ride to the creek didn't take long. They had to hop off their bikes and carefully cross the shallow water, holding their bikes high to avoid getting them soaked. The water was cold, but it felt refreshing in the heat of the day. Their shoes squelched in the mud as they climbed out on the other side, giggling at their muddy footprints.

"This is the part no one knows about," Javi said, his voice full of mystery as they pushed their bikes up the rocky path beyond the creek. "The grown-ups all forget about it, but it's still here, just waiting for someone to find it."

The path grew rougher as they went, and Max, leading the way, had to stop a few times to push aside branches and climb over fallen logs. "This is it," he called back to the others, his voice full of excitement. "We're getting close."

Sam looked around nervously. The trees were taller here, their branches twisting together overhead to block out some of the sunlight. It made the air cooler, but also more still, as if the world was holding its breath.

As they rounded a bend in the path, the trees suddenly gave way, and there it was—the field. The Dump, as some people called it. But to Max, it was much more than that.

"Whoa," Max breathed, stepping forward and letting his bike drop to the ground.

The field was enormous. Tall grass swayed in the breeze, and the ground was uneven, covered in dirt mounds and piles of rocks. In the distance, they could see rusty, abandoned construction equipment—bulldozers, old concrete pipes, and long-forgotten stacks of wood. It was as if the workers had left in the middle of the job and nature had slowly started to take over.

"It's perfect," Jennifer whispered, her eyes wide as she took it all in. "We could build anything here."

Javi was already racing ahead, his bike bouncing over the uneven ground as he whooped with joy. "This is amazing! We could have bike races, build a fort, maybe even set up a zipline or something!"

Sam stood still, taking it all in. There was something almost magical about the place, hidden away from the rest of the world. It was like stepping into a secret land, a place that belonged to them and them alone. "It's like... like it was waiting for us," he said quietly.

Max, not one to stand still for long, clambered up one of the dirt mounds, looking out over the field like a king surveying his kingdom. "This is it," he called down to his friends, a grin spreading across his face. "This is where we'll have our summer."

Jennifer was already gathering pieces of wood and scrap metal, her mind buzzing with ideas. "We could build a fort," she said, already imagining the possibilities. "Something no one could ever knock down. We could make it huge, with towers and secret rooms."

Max jumped down from the mound, landing with a thud. "Exactly. We'll build the biggest, best fort this town has ever seen."

Sam adjusted his glasses, his mind already turning over the logistics. "We'll need supplies. Tools. And we should definitely come up with a design before we start building."

"First things first," Max said, sticking a stick into the ground like a flag. "This field is ours now."

The others gathered around, a sense of excitement hanging in the air. It felt like they were standing on the edge of something big, something that would change their whole summer.

Max grinned at his friends, his heart racing with the thrill of discovery. "From this day forward, this field belongs to the Sunflower Squad."

They cheered, their voices echoing across the empty field. It was just the beginning, but in that moment, they knew one thing for sure: This summer was going to be unforgettable.

CHAPTER 2

THE SUNFLOWER SQUAD

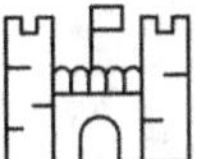

As the Squad stood together, looking out over the vast field that now belonged to them, Max was the first to speak.

"So, what do we build first?" he asked, hands on his hips as he surveyed the open space. "A fort? Or maybe a lookout tower?"

Javi grinned, still balancing his bike against one of the scraggly trees. "A lookout tower with a zipline! That would be amazing."

Sam, kneeling on the ground to pick up some loose twigs, shook his head. "We need to make sure whatever we build is sturdy. We don't want it falling apart the first time it rains."

Jennifer, ever practical, gave a nod as she examined the area. "Sam's right. We can't just throw things together. We need a solid foundation."

Max frowned playfully. "You two always want to think things through. Where's the fun in planning things out? We should just see where it goes."

"There's plenty of fun in not getting buried under a collapsing fort," Sam replied with a smirk, and the others laughed.

Jennifer walked over to a large, flat patch of ground and placed her hands on her hips. "This looks like the best spot to start. It's close to the dirt mounds and flat enough for a sturdy base."

Max picked up a piece of scrap wood lying nearby and tossed it aside, clearing some space. "Good call. We can at least start clearing the area today."

As they worked together, moving branches and bits of old junk to the edge of the field, they started to think about some of their old adventures. Max, as usual, led the charge, while Javi made sure to add a dose of excitement to every idea.

"Hey, Max," Javi said, tossing a rock to the side. "Remember when we tried to build that treehouse in your backyard? No nails, no screws—just wood and string."

Max laughed. "Yeah, and the whole thing collapsed the minute I climbed in. I thought for sure I broke my arm."

"That's because you guys were building it all wrong," Jennifer teased, brushing dirt off her hands. "If I had been there, I would've made sure it stayed up."

Jennifer had moved into the neighborhood two summers earlier, and from the moment she showed Max and Javi how to fix their rickety bike ramp, they knew she was the real deal. Since then, she'd become the group's go-to builder.

"Good thing we've got you now," Javi said, grinning. "Otherwise, this fort would be as much of a disaster as that treehouse."

Sam, stacking pieces of wood into a neat pile, chimed in. "At least Max didn't try to drag me into his treehouse project back then. I barely survived him convincing me to come out of my house to ride bikes."

Max grinned and shrugged. "You needed to get out, Sam. Books are great and all, but you were missing out on real adventures."

Sam gave a small smile as he straightened his glasses. It was true—when he'd moved to the neighborhood two years before, Max had been the one to knock on his door and pull him into their group. At first, Sam wasn't sure he'd fit in, but before long, he found himself joining in on all of their schemes.

Jennifer gestured to the cleared area. "Alright, this spot's looking good. We'll need more supplies, though—wood, nails, rope. We can start on the foundation tomorrow."

Sam nodded, already thinking ahead. "I can work on a blueprint tonight. If we're going to build this fort, it has to be strong."

Max clapped his hands together. "Perfect! Sunflower Squad, we meet here first thing tomorrow morning."

Javi piped up, his grin widening. "And I'll bring snacks. You can't build a fort on an empty stomach! I'll grab some chips and cookies from the kitchen. We'll need all the energy we can get."

Max chuckled. "Good thinking, Javi. Fort-building fuel."

Jennifer rolled her eyes, but there was a smile on her face. "Just make sure you actually do some building and don't just eat the whole time."

"Yeah, we'll work," Javi said, holding up his hands in mock surrender. "But you can't deny that snacks make everything better."

As they finished clearing the area, the field started to feel more like their own. With every piece of junk moved aside and every scrap of wood they gathered, they could picture their fort rising from the ground. It was just the beginning, but it already felt like something special.

"Alright," Max said, glancing at the sky as it began to turn a deep shade of orange. "Let's head back before it gets dark. We've got a lot to do tomorrow."

They grabbed their bikes, still buzzing with excitement, and pedaled away from the field, eager for what the next day would bring.

***

As they neared their street, something caught Sam's eye. "Who's that?" he asked, nodding toward a figure leaning against a tree on the corner.

The others followed his gaze and saw Michael. He was older than them, taller too, with a tough look that made everyone in the neighborhood nervous. He lived in Heathgate, the next suburb over, and he'd built a reputation for causing trouble wherever he went. The kids called him and his group the Heathgate Hooligans—they were always looking to stir things up.

"Just ignore him," Max muttered, gripping his handlebars tighter as they pedaled past. "He's probably just bored."

Michael didn't say anything. He just watched them as they rode by, his eyes narrowing as he noticed their laughter and the dirt on their shoes. The Sunflower Squad was happy—too happy, in his opinion. He hated seeing other kids having fun when he wasn't a part of it.

The four friends didn't look back as they turned down their street and split off to their homes, but Michael stayed where he was, staring after them with a scowl. Something told him they were up to something interesting, and he didn't like being left out.

He kicked a rock and smirked to himself. All he had to do was follow in the direction they'd come from, and he'd find what it was they were trying to hide.

CHAPTER 3

THE RIVAL CREW

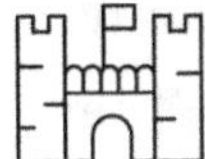

The next morning, the Squad gathered by the creek, their bikes lined up neatly against the trees. Max, Javi, Sam, and Jennifer were all buzzing with excitement, ready to start building the fort they had dreamed up the day before.

Javi balanced a bag of snacks on his handlebars, grinning. "Alright, fort-building fuel has arrived," he announced, shaking the bag so the sound of crinkling chips filled the air.

Jennifer rolled her eyes but smiled. "Let's just make sure we get some actual building done too, okay?"

Max couldn't wait to get started. He rubbed his hands together, already thinking about the fort's shape and how high they could build it. "Alright, Sunflower Squad, let's get to it!"

They pedaled down the familiar path, crossing the creek and heading straight for the field. The morning air was cool, and the sunlight streamed through the trees, making everything feel fresh and new.

When they arrived at the field, something caught Max's eye. Off to one side, near the edge of the dirt mounds, a group of kids was lounging around, looking like they didn't have a care in the world. It was Michael and his crew—the Heathgate Hooligans.

Michael was leaning against his bike with a bored expression, while Erik was tossing a rock from hand to hand. Jessica and Andres sat nearby, talking in low voices. They hadn't noticed the Sunflower Squad yet.

Max's heart sank, but he forced himself to keep pedaling. "Let's just ignore them," he muttered to the others.

Jennifer glanced over at the group, her eyes narrowing. "What are they even doing here?"

"Doesn't matter," Sam said quietly. "We've got our own work to do. Let's just stick to the plan."

The four friends hopped off their bikes and started unpacking their supplies. They tried their best to act normal, even though they could feel the eyes of the Hooligans on them.

For a while, things seemed fine. The Sunflower Squad cleared more space for their fort and started laying out some of the wood they'd collected. Javi was snacking on a bag of chips, trying to keep the mood light, and Sam was already sketching out the next part of their blueprint.

But the uneasy feeling in the air only grew. Max could feel it, like a storm was brewing just out of sight.

Then, out of nowhere, a rock came sailing through the air and landed with a dull thud right next to Javi's feet. He jumped back, startled, dropping his bag of chips.

"What the—?" Javi said, looking around.

They all turned to see Erik smirking, his hand still outstretched from the throw. Jessica laughed, and Michael looked on with a lazy grin.

Max's eyes narrowed. "Okay, that's it."

He stood up, brushing the dirt from his knees, and marched over toward the Hooligans. Jennifer, Javi, and Sam followed close behind.

"Hey!" Max called, stopping a few feet from Michael's group. "What's your problem?"

Michael glanced up lazily, barely acknowledging Max's presence. "Problem? No problem here."

"You just threw a rock at us," Jennifer said, her voice sharp. "We're trying to build something over here, and you're messing with us."

Michael shrugged. "We're just hanging out. Didn't realize you owned the place."

Max clenched his fists, but he held his ground. "We were here first. This field is ours."

Jessica snorted, folding her arms. "Oh, really? I don't see your name on it."

Max's frustration bubbled over. "We've been working on this fort since yesterday. You can't just show up and act like you own the place."

Michael finally stood up, giving Max a cold look. "Look, we don't care about your little fort. We're just here, alright? Maybe we stay, maybe we go. Who knows?"

Andres, fiddling with some fireworks in his pocket, grinned. "Yeah. No big deal, right?"

The tension hung thick in the air, and for a moment, it seemed like the situation might escalate. Max didn't back down, but he could sense that a full-blown argument would only make things worse.

Michael smirked, clearly enjoying the power he held over the group. But then, just as suddenly as it had started, his expression softened into one of indifference. "Whatever. Do what you want. We don't really care."

He turned and motioned to his crew. "Come on. Let's get out of here."

Erik tossed another rock into the dirt, but this time it was a lazy, half-hearted throw. "Yeah, let's go."

The Hooligans mounted their bikes and pedaled off without another word, leaving them standing there, unsure of what had just happened.

Max let out a breath. "What was that about?" he muttered.

Jennifer crossed her arms, watching the Hooligans disappear down the road. "They're messing with us. They want us to think they don't care, but I bet they'll be back."

Javi frowned. "Do you think they'll try to take the field?"

Sam bit his lip, glancing down at the scattered supplies. "Maybe. Or worse—they could mess up everything we've done."

Max's jaw tightened. "Let them try. We're not giving up this field. It's ours, and we're going to build the best fort this town has ever seen."

Jennifer nodded. "Right. Let's focus on that. If they come back, we'll deal with it."

The Squad turned their attention back to the field, each of them wondering if the Hooligans would return—and what would happen if they did. But they couldn't worry about that now. They had a fort to build.

Max, determined not to let the Hooligans ruin their day, grabbed a piece of wood and set it down with purpose. "Alright, let's get to work. This fort isn't going to build itself."

The others followed his lead, working hard to put their plans into action. But even as they worked, the uneasy feeling lingered. The field was theirs—for now—but they all knew that this wasn't the last they'd see of Michael and his crew.

CHAPTER 4

THE RACE TO BUILD

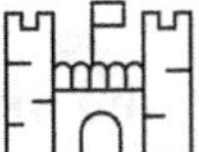

The next day, the Squad was back at the creek, ready for another full day of building. Javi had brought even more snacks, and Sam carried a toolbox his dad had let him borrow. Max was buzzing with excitement, his mind racing with ideas for how to expand the fort.

"We're going to make it huge," Max said, his eyes gleaming as they crossed the creek and pedaled toward the field. "A second level, a lookout post, and maybe even a secret passage."

Jennifer grinned, already picturing the blueprint in her mind. "Let's start with the foundation first. Then we can talk about secret passages."

But when they arrived at the field, Max stopped short. His bike wobbled as he slammed on the brakes.

"What the...?" Max's voice trailed off, his heart sinking.

The fort they had started building the day before was in ruins. The wooden beams they had carefully arranged were scattered, some of them broken in half. Their neatly stacked pile of supplies was overturned, and a few pieces of wood had been snapped and kicked into the dirt. It was as if someone had come through and wrecked everything.

Jennifer's jaw tightened. "They sabotaged us."

Javi let out a low whistle. "I can't believe this."

Sam stood frozen, clutching the handle of his toolbox. "They really did it..."

Max's fists clenched at his sides, anger rising in his chest. He didn't need to ask who had done this. He already knew.

As if on cue, the sound of bikes approaching reached their ears. Max turned just in time to see Michael and the rest of the Hooligans pedaling toward them, grins plastered across their faces.

"Well, well," Michael said, stopping his bike just a few feet away. "Looks like someone's fort wasn't as strong as they thought."

Erik snickered. "Yeah, shame about that."

Max took a step forward, his fists still balled at his sides. "You did this."

Michael shrugged, his smirk widening. "Did what? It's not our fault if your fort can't stand up on its own."

"We know you trashed it," Jennifer snapped, stepping up beside Max. "Don't pretend like you didn't."

Jessica, standing next to Michael, folded her arms. "What's the big deal? It wasn't much of a fort anyway."

Javi's face reddened with frustration. "You had no right!"

Andres, who had been silently watching, finally spoke up. "Look, we're not going to sit here and argue about some crummy fort. This field is big enough for both of us."

Max's eyes narrowed. "No way. We're not sharing this field with you."

Michael's grin faltered slightly, but only for a second. "Fine. Then let's settle this the right way."

Max crossed his arms. "What do you mean?"

Michael leaned forward on his bike. "A challenge. You build your fort, and we'll build ours. Whoever has the best fort by the end of the week gets to keep the field."

Jennifer raised an eyebrow. "What's to stop you from sabotaging us again?"

Michael smirked. "That's the thing. No sabotage, no pranks. Just a straight-up competition. Best fort wins."

Max exchanged a glance with the others. Javi looked excited, Sam looked worried, and Jennifer's expression was unreadable.

But Max's anger was still simmering, and the idea of beating the Hooligans at their own game felt like the perfect way to settle this.

"You're on," Max said, his voice steady.

Michael gave a lazy salute. "Good luck, Sunflower Squad. You're going to need it."

With that, Michael and the Hooligans pedaled away, leaving the Squad standing among the ruins of their fort.

For a moment, no one spoke. Max's mind was spinning with plans, but the wreckage in front of them felt like a punch to the gut.

Finally, Jennifer broke the silence. "We can still do this."

Max turned to her, surprised by the determination in her voice.

Jennifer nodded. "We'll just rebuild. Better than before. We've got the whole week, and we're not going to let them win."

Javi grinned, the fire returning to his eyes. "Yeah, we've got this. We can build the biggest, most awesome fort this field has ever seen!"

Sam still looked uncertain, but he nodded. "We'll need to work fast. And this time, we'll make sure everything's strong enough to hold up."

Max felt the tension ease slightly. His friends weren't giving up, and neither was he.

"Alright," Max said, his voice full of resolve. "Let's show them what we can do."

They spent the rest of the day clearing the wreckage and starting from scratch. It wasn't easy, but the challenge had sparked something in them. By the time the sun started to dip below the horizon, the foundation of their new fort was stronger, more carefully constructed. The Sunflower Squad had a plan, and they were ready to win.

As they worked, Max glanced over at the other side of the field, where the Heathgate Hooligans were setting up their own fort. He squinted, trying to make out what they were doing. To his relief, the Hooligans hadn't made much progress. They were sitting around, tossing rocks, and talking, with only a couple of logs piled together.

"They haven't even started yet," Max muttered under his breath.

Javi, who had noticed too, smirked. "Looks like they're more talk than action."

Jennifer nodded. "Good. That gives us an advantage."

Even Sam, who had been the most nervous about the bet, looked a little more confident. "If we keep this pace, we can finish our fort before they even get started."

Max's determination grew. "We're going to beat them."

As the sun sank lower, the Squad took a step back to admire their work. The foundation of their fort was stronger, better planned, and sturdier than it had been before. It wasn't much yet, but it was the start of something great.

As they packed up their tools and prepared to head home, Max looked over at the field one last time. The challenge had been set. The Hooligans might have trashed their fort, but they were ready to fight back the only way they knew how—by building something incredible.

"This is it," Max said quietly to himself as they pedaled away. "We're going to win this."

CHAPTER 5

ADVENTURES AND ROCKETS

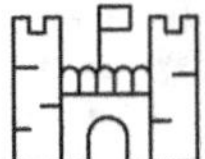

The next few days were a whirlwind of building, racing, and planning for the Squad. Each morning, Max, Jennifer, Javi, and Sam met at the creek, excited to get back to work. Their fort was coming together piece by piece, and even though it was hard work, they knew they were getting closer to something great.

Max stood back, wiping sweat from his forehead as he admired the frame they'd built. "It's looking good," he said, a hint of pride in his voice. "A few more days, and we'll have the best fort in town."

"We need to reinforce the second level before we do anything else," Jennifer pointed out, glancing over the blueprint Sam had drawn up. "If we don't, it could collapse."

Javi, munching on another bag of chips, looked over at the wood pile. "We've got enough for the supports, right?"

Sam nodded. "Yeah, but we'll need to be careful. The higher we go, the more weight it's going to need to hold."

Max grinned. "Good thing we've got a solid team. We'll make sure it holds."

They spent the next few hours hammering beams together, making sure the structure was strong enough to hold their planned lookout tower. Despite the hard work, there was an undeniable buzz of excitement in the air.

As the sun climbed higher in the sky, they took a break, gathering under the shade of a nearby tree to rest. Javi handed out snacks, and they sat back, catching their breath.

"I wonder how the Hooligans are doing," Sam mused, glancing across the field.

Max leaned back against the tree, squinting over at the other side of the field. The Heathgate Hooligans had made some progress, but it wasn't much. From what they could see, Michael and his crew had barely built up the walls of their fort, and it looked shaky at best.

"Not much," Max said, grinning. "We've got them beat already."

Javi chuckled. "Figures. They're all talk."

Jennifer, however, was a little more cautious. "Don't underestimate them. They could pull something together last minute."

Max shrugged, but deep down he knew Jennifer was right. The Hooligans weren't to be trusted, especially when it came to playing fair.

"Let's not get too comfortable," Max said, sitting up. "We still have a lot to do."

But before they could get back to work, Javi jumped up, his eyes sparkling with mischief. "Before we start again, how about a quick race?"

"A race?" Sam asked, raising an eyebrow. "On bikes?"

"Yeah!" Javi said, already grabbing his bike. "Come on, we've been building all morning. Let's have some fun!"

Max grinned. "You're on."

Jennifer rolled her eyes, but she smiled too. "Alright, fine. But just one race."

The four of them mounted their bikes and lined up at the edge of the field. The makeshift racecourse they had mapped out the day before wound through the trees and around the mounds of dirt, full of twists and turns that promised an exciting challenge.

"First one back to the fort wins!" Javi shouted, pedaling forward before anyone had a chance to react.

"Hey! No fair!" Max yelled, laughing as he kicked off after him.

Jennifer and Sam followed, their laughter echoing through the trees as they sped around corners and over bumps. The air was filled with the sounds of tires skidding on dirt, shouts of encouragement, and playful jostling as they all tried to outpace each other.

Javi took the lead, darting between the trees with ease, but Max was right on his tail. Jennifer was keeping up, her focus sharp, while Sam, cautious as ever, took the turns a little slower.

As they approached the final stretch, Max pedaled harder, closing the gap between him and Javi. Just as he was about to pass, Javi swerved, cutting him off with a grin.

"No way you're beating me, Max!" Javi called over his shoulder.

But Max wasn't giving up. With a final burst of speed, he managed to pass Javi just before crossing the finish line, skidding to a stop in front of their fort.

"I win!" Max shouted, breathless but grinning from ear to ear.

Javi pulled up beside him, shaking his head with a laugh. "I was so close!"

Jennifer arrived next, rolling her eyes but smiling. "You two are impossible."

Sam came in last, panting as he stopped his bike. "Maybe next time we can have a race that doesn't involve nearly crashing into trees."

"Where's the fun in that?" Javi teased, ruffling Sam's hair.

As they caught their breath, Max glanced over at the Hooligans' side of the field again. Michael and his crew were still working, but it looked like they were having trouble getting their walls to stand straight.

Max couldn't help but feel a sense of satisfaction. They were ahead, and with the way things were going, they would win the challenge easily.

But just as they were about to get back to work, something unexpected happened.

A loud whoosh filled the air, followed by a sharp crackle. The Sunflower Squad turned to see a small rocket shoot up from the Hooligans' side of the field, trailing smoke behind it.

"What in the world?" Javi exclaimed, shading his eyes as he looked up at the rocket.

The Hooligans were laughing, watching as their homemade rocket soared into the sky. Michael, with his arms crossed, looked smug, clearly pleased with himself.

"They've got rockets?" Sam asked, wide-eyed.

Max frowned. "Looks like it."

Jennifer crossed her arms. "They're trying to show off. But a rocket isn't going to win them the challenge."

"They're probably just trying to distract us," Max added, watching as the rocket fizzled out and fell back to the ground.

For a moment, the Squad stood there, unsure of what to make of the Hooligans' stunt. It was flashy, sure, but it didn't change the fact that their fort was barely holding together.

Max turned back to his friends, his determination growing. "Let's not get sidetracked. We've got a fort to finish."

Jennifer nodded. "Yeah, we've got this."

As they got back to work, Max couldn't shake the feeling that the Hooligans were up to something. They might have rockets, but his squad had something better—a plan.

CHAPTER 6

TENSION AND SABOTAGE

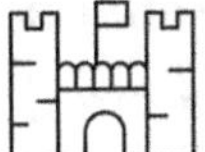

The week was flying by, and both groups were racing to finish their forts before the deadline. The Squad worked tirelessly, adding walls, reinforcing beams, and making sure everything was strong. But even though they were focused, strange things started happening—things they couldn't explain.

It started small. One morning, they arrived at the field to find their neatly stacked woodpile scattered all over the place. Jennifer frowned, scratching her head. "I know we stacked this last night. It didn't just fall over."

Max shrugged it off. "Maybe the wind knocked it down."

Javi wasn't convinced. "Or maybe the Hooligans came by after we left."

Sam looked around nervously. "You really think they're sneaking around our fort at night?"

"I don't know," Javi replied, his voice low. "But it wouldn't surprise me. They'd do anything to win."

Max shook his head. "We don't have time to worry about them. Let's just rebuild the pile and get back to work."

They worked hard that day, but the uneasy feeling lingered. And it wasn't long before something else went wrong.

The next afternoon, while Jennifer was securing the roof beams, the rope they were using suddenly snapped. Jennifer fell backward into the dirt, landing hard on the ground.

"Jennifer!" Sam shouted, rushing over to help her up.

"I'm fine," Jennifer said, dusting herself off. "But this rope—it's not frayed. It looks like it was cut."

Max inspected the rope, his brow furrowed. "I knew it. They're messing with us."

Javi scowled. "They've been sneaking around, I bet. Trying to slow us down."

"We don't know for sure," Sam said, his voice quiet. "It could just be old rope. Or maybe the weather—it's been windy the last couple of days."

Max wasn't buying it. "No way. This isn't a coincidence."

As the Squad tried to make sense of what was happening, things on the Hooligans' side weren't going any better. That same afternoon, a loud crash echoed across the field. Max and his friends turned just in time to see the Hooligans' fort collapse in a pile of wooden beams and dust.

Michael stormed over, his eyes blazing with anger. "What did you do?"

Max blinked, caught off guard. "What are you talking about?"

"Don't play dumb," Erik snarled, standing beside Michael. "We know you messed with our fort. It didn't just fall down by itself."

Jennifer crossed her arms. "We haven't touched your fort. We've been too busy fixing the mess you made of ours."

Michael's expression darkened. "You think you're funny, huh? First, our wood goes missing, and now our whole fort collapses? This has your name all over it."

Max's frustration flared. "You're blaming us for your mistakes? Maybe if you knew how to build properly, your fort wouldn't be falling apart."

Michael stepped forward, his face tight with frustration. "We know you've been sabotaging us."

"Look," Jennifer said, stepping between the two groups, her voice calm but firm. "We didn't touch your fort. You've had problems just like us. Maybe something else is going on."

Michael's fists unclenched, but his face was still full of suspicion. "Like what?"

Sam hesitated. "Well... what if neither of us is sabotaging the other?"

Javi snorted. "What are you saying, Sam? That the wind is sabotaging us?"

Sam shrugged, but he looked uneasy. "I don't know, but it's strange, right? Both of our forts are having problems. Maybe it's just bad luck, or... something else."

For a moment, both groups stood in silence, unsure of what to think. The tension hung in the air, thick and heavy.

Finally, Michael let out a long breath. "Fine. Maybe you didn't touch our fort. But if I find out you're lying..."

Max's eyes narrowed. "Same goes for you."

Without another word, Michael turned and stomped back toward his collapsed fort, Erik and the others following close behind. The Squad watched them go, frustration simmering beneath the surface.

"This is getting ridiculous," Javi muttered, kicking at the dirt. "We've got our own problems, and they're blaming us for theirs."

Sam nodded. "Yeah, but what if it's something else? What if there's someone—or something—messing with both of us?"

Jennifer frowned. "Like what?"

"I don't know," Sam admitted. "But this doesn't feel right."

Max sighed, running a hand through his hair. "We don't have time to figure this out. We've only got a couple of days left. We need to focus on finishing our fort."

Jennifer nodded, her expression determined. "Agreed. If we finish strong, none of this sabotage—whatever it is—will matter."

Javi grinned, his usual confidence returning. "We'll beat them. Our fort's way better than theirs."

Max glanced over at the Hooligans, who were scrambling to fix the mess they'd made of their fort. A part of him still wanted to believe that Michael and his crew were behind the sabotage, but Sam's words kept echoing in his mind. Could it really be something else?

As they worked late into the afternoon, they kept their heads down, focused on the task at hand. The wind picked up, rustling the trees around them, and dark clouds gathered on the horizon, signaling an approaching storm.

Max looked up at the sky, feeling the weight of the deadline pressing down on them. "We've got to finish this," he muttered. "No matter what's going on, we need to win."

Jennifer hammered another nail into the beam. "We will. Let's just stay focused."

But as the sun dipped below the horizon and they packed up for the day, a sense of unease lingered in the air. Something strange was happening at the field, and neither group knew how it would end.

CHAPTER 7

THE STAKEOUT

The week was nearing its end, and the pressure was mounting for both the Squad and the Hooligans. With only a couple of days left before the deadline to finish their forts, the strange sabotage continued. Every morning, Max and his friends arrived to find something broken or out of place at their fort.

"It's got to be them," Javi muttered as he tightened a bolt on their lookout post. "Who else would be sneaking around here?"

Max hammered another nail into the beam and sighed. "It makes sense. But how do we catch them in the act?"

Jennifer, balancing on a ladder while reinforcing a roof beam, glanced over at the Hooligans' side of the field. "If they're sneaking around at night, we'll need to catch them while they're doing it."

Sam looked up from the blueprint, nervous but intrigued. "You mean, like a stakeout?"

Javi's eyes lit up. "Exactly. We stake out the fort tonight and catch them red-handed."

Max nodded, his mind racing with the possibilities. "We'll pretend to leave but come back once it's dark. If they're up to something, we'll see it."

Jennifer climbed down from the ladder, wiping her hands. "If we do this, we need to hide somewhere they won't see us."

"I know the perfect spot," Max said, pointing to a cluster of thick bushes near the edge of the field. "We can see everything from there without being noticed."

As the sun began to set, the Squad finished their work for the day and packed up as if they were going home. They waved at each other and pedaled away from the field, pretending the day was over.

But once they were out of sight, they doubled back, parking their bikes a little further down the road and sneaking quietly back to the field.

Max motioned for everyone to stay low as they crawled into the bushes. "Keep quiet," he whispered. "We wait and see what they do."

The night air grew cooler as the moon rose, casting long shadows over the field. The Squad crouched in the bushes, eyes fixed on the Hooligans' side of the field. Time dragged on slowly, and the only sounds were the occasional rustling of leaves and the distant chirping of crickets.

"I hope they show up soon," Javi whispered, stifling a yawn. "I didn't bring enough snacks for this."

"They'll come," Max muttered, his eyes scanning the dark field. "They have to."

But as the hours passed, nothing happened. There was no sign of the Hooligans sneaking around. The field remained quiet, almost too quiet.

"I don't get it," Sam whispered. "Where are they?"

"They're probably waiting for us to sabotage their fort," Jennifer replied, her voice low. "They're doing a stakeout too."

Javi chuckled softly. "So they're hiding from us while we're hiding from them? This is ridiculous."

Max frowned. "Maybe they're planning something for later."

Before anyone could respond, a sudden flash of light caught Max's attention. A faint beam of a flashlight flickered from the other side of the field, cutting through the darkness.

"There!" Max whispered urgently. "They're here."

They peered through the bushes, trying to make out what was happening. Sure enough, they could see the Hooligans standing near their fort, huddled together with their flashlights, whispering quietly.

"I thought for sure they'd be here by now," Erik muttered, his voice just loud enough for the Squad to hear.

"They're probably watching us," Michael replied, shining his flashlight around the field. "Waiting for us to leave."

Jennifer raised an eyebrow. "They're doing the same thing we are."

Max's eyes widened. "They think we're going to sabotage them."

Javi stifled a laugh. "This is ridiculous. We're both out here hiding from each other."

"Do we talk to them?" Sam asked quietly, glancing at Max.

Max hesitated. Part of him wanted to confront the Hooligans and clear things up, but the rivalry between their groups still ran deep. Instead, he motioned for everyone to stay down. "Not yet. Let's see if they leave."

The Squad stayed hidden, watching the Hooligans move around, clearly as frustrated and restless as they were. After what felt like forever, Michael finally sighed. "This is pointless. Let's just call it a night."

The Hooligans gathered their things and, after another quick scan of the field, headed off toward their bikes, disappearing into the night.

Max let out a breath of relief. "Okay, they're gone. Let's get out of here."

The Squad quietly crawled out of the bushes, stretching their tired limbs as they stood up. Just as they were about to leave, Sam stopped, his ears perking up at a faint rustling sound coming from the trees nearby.

"Did you hear that?" Sam whispered, looking toward the bushes.

The others froze, listening carefully. But the rustling stopped, and everything was silent again.

"It's probably just the wind," Javi said, waving it off. "Let's get out of here."

Sam hesitated for a moment, still staring at the bushes, but eventually nodded. "Yeah, I guess you're right."

As they pedaled away from the field, Max couldn't shake the feeling that something was off. They hadn't seen the Hooligans sabotage anything, and yet, their fort kept getting messed up.

"All this time, and we still haven't caught them," Max muttered, frustrated. "What if we're missing something?"

Jennifer shrugged. "We'll find out soon enough. We just have to keep our heads down and finish the fort."

As they rode toward home, the wind rustled the trees behind them, and Sam glanced back one last time. The sound had seemed different somehow—almost like something was watching them—but he shook the thought away. It was late, and his mind was playing tricks on him.

Tomorrow, they'd figure it out.

CHAPTER 8

THE ROCKET LAUNCH

With only two days left before the deadline to finish their forts, the Squad arrived at the field, eager to make the most of the time they had left. Despite the setbacks, their fort was coming together well, and Max was determined to finish strong.

"We need to get that roof on today," Jennifer said, looking over the blueprint. "If we do that, we'll be ahead."

Sam nodded as he sorted through the tools. "And we'll need to reinforce the walls, too."

They started working, but as they made their way through the morning, something felt off. Max looked around the field, his brow furrowing. Everything seemed fine, but he couldn't help but feel that the strange events from the past few days weren't over yet.

His suspicion was confirmed when they went to grab more wood from their pile, only to find it scattered all over the ground again.

"You've got to be kidding me," Max muttered, shaking his head. "Not again."

Jennifer knelt down, inspecting the pile. "We stacked this up yesterday before we left."

"This doesn't make any sense," Sam added. "We were all here last night. It wasn't them."

Javi, who had been tying down one of the beams, stood up and looked over at the Hooligans' fort. "You don't think they're still messing with us, do you?"

Max shook his head. "I don't think so. They've had problems too. Why would they sabotage us and themselves?"

The group stood in silence, each of them trying to figure out what was going on. Whatever had been happening, it clearly wasn't either of them causing the trouble.

"We need to get to the bottom of this," Jennifer said. "Something's going on, and it's not just bad luck."

As they restacked the wood, the sound of voices from the Hooligans' side caught their attention. Andres was fiddling with a rocket launcher, clearly frustrated as Michael and Erik watched from nearby.

"They're still working on those rockets," Sam observed. "Looks like they're having trouble again."

Max watched for a moment, then glanced at Sam. "You know how to fix that, right?"

Sam nodded, adjusting his glasses. "I think so. I could help."

Max hesitated, then shrugged. "Let's go. Maybe if we help them, we can figure out what's really been going on."

The Squad made their way across the field, stopping a few feet from the Hooligans' fort. Andres looked up, surprised to see them.

"Need some help with that rocket?" Sam asked, nodding toward the launcher.

Michael's eyes narrowed. "Why are you over here?"

"We're not here to mess with you," Max said. "Sam knows how to fix rockets, and it looks like you're having trouble."

Andres sighed, clearly frustrated. "Yeah, the stupid thing won't launch. We've tried everything."

Without saying a word, Sam stepped forward, crouching down to inspect the rocket's wiring. After a few minutes of adjusting the connections, he smiled and stepped back. "That should do it. Try now."

Andres hesitated, then hit the launch button. With a loud whoosh, the rocket shot up into the sky, trailing a plume of smoke as it soared above the field.

"It worked!" Jessica said, her eyes wide.

Both groups watched as the rocket flew upward, but it didn't go far before it started its descent, falling back down toward a patch of trees near the edge of the field.

"We should see where it landed," Andres said, already grabbing his bike.

Michael nodded, and the two groups, without hesitation, hopped on their bikes and sped toward the trees.

When they reached the landing spot, something unexpected caught Jennifer's eye. Scattered among the bushes were some of the tools they had been missing over the past few days—hammers, wrenches, and pieces of rope, all piled up beneath a small tree.

"Look at this," Jennifer said, picking up one of the hammers. "These are ours."

Max stepped closer, his eyes widening. "So, this is where all our missing stuff went."

Before anyone could react, a rustling sound came from the bushes. Everyone froze, their eyes darting toward the noise.

Out from behind the bushes scurried a raccoon, clutching a piece of rope in its tiny paws. It darted across the clearing and disappeared into a hollow log. Moments later, two more raccoons appeared, each carrying small bits of wood and metal.

Michael stared, his mouth open. "You've got to be kidding me."

"It's them," Javi muttered, shaking his head in disbelief. "They've been messing with our forts."

The two groups watched as the raccoons rummaged through the pile of stolen tools, tugging at the ropes and playing with the wood. It was clear now—these mischievous creatures had been the ones sabotaging both forts, not the kids.

"All this time..." Max began, shaking his head.

"We've been blaming each other for nothing," Jennifer finished.

Sam chuckled softly. "And all along, it was just raccoons messing with us."

Michael crossed his arms, looking both annoyed and relieved. "Well, that explains why the sabotage kept happening."

Javi picked up one of the wrenches, grinning. "We should've done a stakeout on these guys instead of each other."

Andres laughed. "Seriously! We wasted a whole night thinking you were sneaking around, and it turns out it was these little guys."

Both groups stood there for a moment, the weight of their rivalry starting to lift. They had been caught in a misunderstanding, and now the truth was finally out.

"Well," Jennifer said, stepping forward, "we've still got forts to finish. But now that we know the raccoons were behind everything, maybe we can stop blaming each other."

Max glanced at Michael, raising an eyebrow. "What do you think? No more sabotage?"

Michael hesitated, then nodded. "Yeah. We've been blaming each other for too long."

As they all gathered up the tools, there was an undeniable shift in the air. The tension that had once hung between them seemed to dissolve, replaced by an easy camaraderie.

"Think about it," Max said as they headed back to the field. "If we work together, we could make both forts even better."

Michael looked at him thoughtfully. "Maybe."

When they returned to their side of the field, Max couldn't help but feel that the rivalry had finally started to fade. The raccoons may have caused all the trouble, but in the end, they had also brought the two groups closer together.

As they parted ways to continue their work, the Squad and the Hooligans both knew one thing for sure: the next day would be different.

CHAPTER 9

TOGETHER IS BETTER

The next morning, the Squad arrived at the field feeling lighter than they had in days. Now that they knew the real culprits behind the sabotage were the raccoons, it seemed like the rivalry between them and the Heathgate Hooligans was finally starting to fade.

As they unpacked their tools and began getting back to work, Max spotted Michael and the Hooligans on the other side of the field, already starting on their fort.

"You think they'll actually want to team up?" Javi asked, hammering a nail into one of the beams.

Max shrugged, his eyes still on the Hooligans. "Maybe. We've all been working so hard, and we've got something great going. If they're serious, we could really make this place awesome."

Jennifer nodded as she measured a piece of wood. "It's worth asking. We've all seen what we can do on our own—imagine what we could do together."

Sam adjusted his glasses, glancing over the blueprint they had drawn up. "We'd have more hands and more ideas. We could even build something bigger than we planned."

Max took a deep breath and waved across the field. "Let's see what they think."

Michael, who had been working on the base of their fort, noticed Max's wave and walked over, followed by Erik, Jessica, and Andres. The tension from earlier in the week seemed to have lifted, but there was still a hint of uncertainty in the air.

"Morning," Michael said, stopping a few feet from Max.

"Morning," Max replied. "We've been thinking. Now that we know neither of us was messing with the forts, maybe we should work together."

Michael crossed his arms, clearly considering the idea. "You mean, like... combine our forts?"

"Exactly," Jennifer chimed in, stepping forward. "We've both built some great stuff already, but if we team up, we can make something even better."

Erik, who had been quiet, scratched his head. "We've got some cool ideas, but we've been stuck on a few things. I guess working together could help."

Sam, always the planner, held up their blueprint. "We've got designs for towers, secret rooms, and a lookout post. But with your ideas, we could make it even bigger."

Jessica smiled. "We've been talking about adding a zipline between two trees. It would be awesome if we had the space."

Javi grinned. "A zipline? I'm all in!"

Michael glanced at his team, then back at Max. "Alright. Let's do it. We'll team up."

Max smiled and extended his hand. "Deal."

Michael shook his hand, and just like that, the Sunflower Squad and the Heathgate Hooligans were officially working together.

The shift in energy was immediate. Both groups quickly came together, brainstorming ideas, combining their strengths, and sharing tools and materials. What had once been a competition became a collaboration, and it didn't take long for the excitement to spread.

Jennifer worked with Jessica and Erik to figure out how to reinforce the lookout post and make it taller. Andres and Javi started mapping out where the zipline would go, arguing playfully over which tree would work best. Sam and Michael took a closer look at the overall structure, deciding where they could add more secret hideaways and strengthen the base.

"We could build a tunnel under this section," Sam suggested, pointing to an area near the edge of the fort. "It'll connect the lookout tower to the main base."

Michael nodded, clearly impressed. "That could work. We've been trying to figure out how to link everything together."

Max was busy organizing the next phase of construction with Erik and Jennifer, hammering down the new beams for the second floor. The more they worked together, the more everyone realized how much easier—and more fun—it was when they combined their ideas and skills.

"Okay, we're going to need more wood for the zipline platform," Andres called out from across the field.

"I'll get it," Javi shouted, already sprinting toward the woodpile.

"Don't forget the rope!" Jessica added, laughing as she helped Jennifer secure the roof beams.

The atmosphere in the field had completely changed. Where there had once been tension and rivalry, there was now laughter, teamwork, and excitement. Both groups were eager to see what they could create together, and the progress was faster than anyone expected.

By the time the sun began to sink lower in the sky, the combined fort had taken shape. It was bigger and better than either group had imagined. The lookout tower now had two levels, the zipline was almost ready, and the secret tunnel Sam had suggested was halfway finished.

Max stood back, wiping his hands on his jeans, and looked at what they had built. "This is amazing."

Michael, standing beside him, nodded in agreement. "Yeah. I didn't think it would turn out this cool."

"We've still got a little more to do tomorrow," Jennifer pointed out, brushing dirt off her hands. "But if we finish strong, this will be the best fort the town's ever seen."

Javi, who was testing the strength of the zipline, grinned. "And we'll have the best lookout post in town."

Sam adjusted his glasses, a satisfied smile on his face. "This is what happens when we work together."

Michael glanced over at Max, his expression thoughtful. "I guess we spent too much time fighting when we could've been building."

Max smiled. "Well, at least now we know what we're capable of."

As the two groups packed up their tools for the day, there was a sense of accomplishment and pride hanging in the air. They had all worked hard—together—and the result was something they could all be proud of.

"Tomorrow, we finish it," Max said, slinging his tool bag over his shoulder.

Michael grinned. "And then it's time for the zipline test."

Javi cheered. "I call first ride!"

Everyone laughed as they grabbed their bikes and pedaled away. Proud that they were almost finished with their forts and filled with a sense of accomplishment after gaining new friends in the process.

CHAPTER 10

ONE BIG ADVENTURE

The Squad and the Hooligans gathered around the fort, eager to put in the last few hours of work. After a week of building, the end was finally in sight. The second level of the lookout tower needed a few more beams, and the zipline, which they had been waiting to test, was ready to go.

"We're almost there," Max said, stepping back to look at the structure. "Just a couple more hours, and we'll be done."

"And I'm definitely going on the zipline first," Javi added, his eyes gleaming with excitement.

They got to work, each kid focused on their task. Michael and Erik secured the last support beams on the lookout tower while Jennifer and Jessica reinforced the ropes. Sam and Andres double-checked the platform for the zipline, making sure everything was sturdy enough for the ride they had all been waiting for.

After two hours of hammering, measuring, and tightening bolts, the fort was finally finished. The second level of the tower stood tall, the zipline gleamed in the sun, and everything looked stronger than ever.

"Looks like we're done," Michael said, taking a step back to admire their work.

Max nodded, his smile growing. "Time for the zipline!"

Javi wasted no time. He scrambled up the ladder to the zipline platform, grinning from ear to ear. "Here we go!" he shouted as he grabbed the handlebar and pushed off.

The zipline whistled as Javi zipped across the field, his laughter echoing behind him. The line stretched from the lookout tower to a tree near the edge of the field, and Javi landed with a smooth skid.

"That was awesome!" he shouted back to the others. "You've all got to try it!"

One by one, the rest of the group took their turns on the zipline, their shouts of excitement filling the air. It was the moment they had all been waiting for, and the zipline didn't disappoint.

When Michael took his turn, he landed near the tree, but as he was dusting himself off, something caught his eye—a patch of dirt that seemed uneven, like something was buried just beneath the surface.

"Hey, guys, come over here!" Michael called out, crouching down to inspect it.

The others rushed over, curious about what he had found.

"What is it?" Max asked as Michael brushed away some of the dirt.

"I don't know, but it looks like something's buried here," Michael replied, digging his fingers into the ground.

With everyone's help, they started to dig, using their hands and small tools to loosen the soil. After a few minutes, the tip of a rusted metal box appeared, partially buried beneath the earth.

"Whoa, it's a chest!" Javi said, his voice filled with excitement. "What do you think's inside?"

They carefully dug the rest of it out and pulled the chest free from the dirt. The old lock had rusted over, but with a little effort, Michael pried it open with a nearby rock.

As the lid creaked open, they all leaned in to see what was inside.

The chest was filled with small trinkets—a worn compass, a pocket watch, old coins, and a weathered piece of parchment that looked like a map. The items were clearly old, but none of the kids knew exactly how old.

"This is so cool," Jessica said, picking up the compass. "But why would all this be buried here?"

Max unfolded the map, his eyes narrowing as he studied the faded lines and symbols. "It looks like some kind of treasure map."

Sam carefully lifted out the pocket watch, turning it over in his hands. "There are initials engraved on this. It must've belonged to someone important."

Jennifer examined the coins, her eyes wide with curiosity. "These could be really valuable. We need to figure out where all this came from."

Michael, still holding the chest, nodded thoughtfully. "We've got to find out what this is all about."

The kids exchanged excited glances. They had come to the field expecting to finish their fort, but instead, they had stumbled upon something mysterious—something that would lead them to their next big adventure.

"We should talk to Mr. Clark when school starts," Sam suggested, referring to their history teacher. "He's always talking about old artifacts and maps. I bet he could help us figure out where this stuff came from."

"And my grandpa collects old things," Michael added. "He might know something about this, too."

Jennifer nodded. "Mr. Clark would be all over this. He loves old stuff."

Max folded the map carefully, his mind racing with possibilities. "We'll bring it to him when school starts. But for now, let's just enjoy the rest of the summer."

The group agreed, feeling the thrill of a new mystery bubbling beneath the surface. The fort may have been finished, but it was clear that their adventure wasn't over yet.

"Let's keep the chest safe for now," Jennifer said, closing the lid and setting it beside the fort. "When school starts, we'll figure out what it all means."

Max grinned, looking around at the fort they had built together. "We've got a lot to figure out, but first—let's make the most of this fort."

As they climbed back up the tower, ready for another round on the zipline, the chest sat quietly in the shade, its secrets waiting to be uncovered.

"Best summer ever," Javi said with a laugh as he zipped across the field once more.

Max glanced back at the chest, a grin spreading across his face. "And it's only the beginning."